Creance

THE DRINKING GOURD CHAPBOOK POETRY PRIZE

SERIES EDITORS

Chris Abani

John Alba Cutler

Reginald Gibbons

Susannah Young-ah Gottlieb

Ed Roberson

Matthew Shenoda

Natasha Trethewey

Creance; or, Comest Thou Cosmic Nazarite

Poems

Andrew E. Colarusso

NORTHWESTERN UNIVERSITY PRESS

EVANSTON, ILLINOIS

creance: (n) *Falconry*; a long fine cord attached to a raptor's leash to prevent escape during training.

Origin: late fifteenth century: from French *créance* ("faith"), also denoting a cord to retain a bird of *peu de créance* ("of little faith," i.e., which cannot yet be relied upon).

Northwestern University Press
www.nupress.northwestern.edu

Northwestern University Poetry and Poetics Colloquium
www.poetry.northwestern.edu

Copyright © 2019 by Andrew E. Colarusso. Foreword copyright © 2019 by Matthew Shenoda. Published 2019 by Northwestern University Press. All rights reserved.

Printed in the United States of America

10 9 8 7 6 5 4 3 2 1

Library of Congress Cataloging-in-Publication Data

Names: Colarusso, Andrew Elias, author. | Shenoda, Matthew, writer of foreword.
Title: Creance, or, Comest thou cosmic Nazarite : poems / Andrew E. Colarusso.
Other titles: Creance | Comest thou cosmic Nazarite |
Drinking gourd chapbook poetry prize.
Description: Evanston, Illinois : Northwestern University Press, 2019. |
Series: Drinking gourd chapbook poetry prize
Identifiers: LCCN 2018036957 | ISBN 9780810140202 (pbk. : alk. paper)
Classification: LCC PS3603.O41235 A6 2019 | DDC 811.6—dc23
LC record available at https://lccn.loc.gov/2018036957

Contents

Foreword

Matthew Shenoda

In *Creance* we are introduced from the very title to the concept of stricture and how it is we come to learn, an idea that brings about notions both of disciplined ability and of a restraint on freedom. Colarusso's poems skillfully play off these tensions, often taking their time moving the reader forward at a contemplative pace, lingering on the small moments that help us come to terms with how we understand and position ourselves in this larger world. His is a meditation on the essential elements of our humanity, on the small movements and quiet moments that reflect our inner spirits and bond us to one another.

Split into sections titled "Southern" and "Northern," *Creance* is simultaneously defined by an American North and South and by a hemispheric sensibility. The geographic binary Colarusso plays with in these two sections feels like an exploration into how similar ideas of difference can be. In the end, his poems center on individuals who might ultimately be found anywhere, and it is his ability to move quickly and deftly into the inner lives of these characters that is both most striking and illustrative of the commonalities his poems arrive at. In "Eleanor," he writes:

> slouched in her seat not asleep
> but bent with regard for a century
> lifts her head looking up to get
> her bearings clutches a pink plush
> to her chest and forgets softness
> into an empty stomach rounding
> vacancy on the greens of her eyes
> after the seasons they disarrange
> like rosary beads her prayers each
> counted if unnumbered as hours
> carry dust

And it is in these "hours carrying dust" that we see the ways in which the existential and the tactile come together to help us make sense of who we are. There is nothing essentialist in these poems, only a yearning for some larger appreciation.

These are poems that the reader needs to sink into, get carried by, and sometimes float away on. They pull us inward and make us think alongside the speaker of the poems, as in "Aleta":

> And I wonder if you know what
> it means to drive through the desert
> not alone, but holding, clutched in
> your left hand, loss. Not alone, but
> sitting beside something outside of
> language, outside of the car, which
> nonetheless breathes in and out a
> sighing reminder of the temporary.

It is in that sense of the temporary where perhaps these poems become most alive, sharing with the reader moments that are earnest and vulnerable, striving for understanding over proclamation.

But this is also a poetry of celebration, of what Colarusso calls "melangaudy," which he defines as "Black joy; delight despite disunion." He revels in quiet moments (often between two people) that help to anchor us and attempt to fuse this notion of disunion. And even more so, he revels in the play of language, in the beating pulse of syntax and the rhythmic movements of syllabics. Often sparse on punctuation, Colarusso lets the language carry the line and sometimes crashes words into one another with the experimental verve of a deft percussionist. His is a poetry at the edge of things, both climbing and peering, and *Creance* is a wonderful primer from an emerging voice that I am certain we will hear more from.

SOUTHERN

❡

Mikhtam

in memory of Aunt Ruth & Uncle Francis

Down a dirt road in a garden of kumquats where
pleasure-boxing with orange the light of Alabama
ribbons through the branches and the clapboard
is warmed its paint peeling. He steps out angling
the tip

Of a bowie knife between his incisors left hand on
his hip cocked and a gold tooth a nooner patina on
his forehead then sheathing the knife he sucks his
teeth loudly and recedes again into the darkness
of the house.

We follow him inside to where a litter gambols
in a pen brindled mutts the size of young hens and
the bitch laid out drawing her breath in submission
looks up aware of why we are here why we dance
with the woman we came with

Who points to the runt covered in nettles the one
sleeping among things who remembers
$\qquad\qquad\qquad$ what most would not.

Monkey Study with Fur

after Solmaz Sharif

I musta been young when I held the gun
not more than ten which meant my sister
had five the way I date my youth that half
decade difference and it was my mother s
snub nose revolver I held surprised
to find the trigger so difficult to pull
way less give than I imagined
worlding the day

Wrote Pessoa in English of primates made
to pray

> *Happy are beasts that can have no faith*
> *Yet if ye taught an ape to [   ] and kneel*
> *And move his lips and join his hands or reel . . .*

perhaps when still the young poet
pining among Kaffirs in Durban
for his King his Fifth Empire and his other selves

> *I doubt not he would have more faith than we.*

The infinitive left blank so to [speak]
or not say the apes are left to [play] on their own
void plane or that to leave blank is to [pray]
properly beyond carnal impossible for the black
body or   (the poem yet unpublished)

Let me show you a monkey raised
on a nursing
wire-
mother

said Dr Harry Harlow noting
for the film crew
that the baby macaque may spend
less than one hour
with nursing wire-mother
and as much as eighteen hours
with fur
sucking its little thumb
like I used to suck my thumb
and I think I think Pessoa was right
about what lives without language
live in a state of perpetual prayer

When I held the gun I held the gun high
and my mother corrected
said no
point it down
        it s not loaded
        but you never know
        she added
to quell the spirits I d lined without looking in its sights

        cause when it s my time to go
        I ll wait for God with the .44

rapped a young Nas in 92

living beings have a certain relation to death,
said Derrida to his students a decade later
(*The Beast & the Sovereign* vol ii p10)

Harlow s monkeys were meant to [say]
something about attachment about choosing
against our best interest but

without fur without touch that affirms you
are not alone not an animal in a cage I know
trust me you ll die before death calls your name

without milk a monkey might die still intact
the inevitability here being this death
less spirit but only monkeys know that

it s not either or

Rachel

in memory of Trayvon Martin

A man tending to his pickup on the lawn
of a Methodist church saw it all and said
nothing, awed. He with his black Stetson
turned away, crossed himself, muttering
not to be confused for prayer. The blood
like galvanized iron beneath the swelling
made it hard to swallow or hard to know
why exactly what happened. So bruised.
The blued cheekbone, lips overripe and
swollen to silence, the hip made raw and
adrenal tremors. Such a dream, the way
a body, gliding across glass, can be still
inside so still. Such a dream, the way a
body can be thrown, all tumult of spirit
and trying to stand an entire memory in
foreshortened light, in the yellow of the
world. I don't know. We stand as if out
of swales came songs of musket fire and
exhaust-like perfume of what is possible
reaching toward the leavened ledge of I
can see for miles, what's coming, what's
behind. You have to make them see you,
she said, when you cross, knowing God
dammit that if the sky turned cadmium
red right now, half the world wouldn't
know. So—you were saying something
about strawberry starbursts?

Melangaudy

MELANGAUDY *adj.*

: Black joy; delight despite disunion

• *It was the melangaudy realization that this woman, whose face held so much light and looked so much like his own, was his mother. "Mommy?" he asked. And she nodded. And they cried.*

ORIGIN:
Greek from *melas, melan-* '**black**,' + Latin from *gaudium* '**joy**'

see also:
MELANGAUDIUM *n.*

Tape

after Nick Terry

Witness to the
ligatures that
keep us moor
ed to meaning
in such a place
as small as this
and narrow. The
door between our
bed and bath—
shivering at night,
and in the sun,
for the summer,
engorged. The
sheer warp of it
all distorting the
frame so that
just this morning
it cracked and
swallowed me
entirely like an
Ephraimite in
Gilead. Gilead.
Then I began to
wonder about
the space that,
needing to be
hinged, begs also
to be adorned.
The only tape   I found was
kept in a drawer   on your side

beneath the bed   and it was
blue.   And I put one
piece   over the crack—
not to fix it,   only so
you'd see.   Then I put
another.   And another.
Until it was   dark out
and you were not here
and the sound of the
door beneath the tape
I stuck up for you
came out like a fury
with the light of the
moon whining through
the blue.

Aleta

What more than hints at, reminds
one of, temporariness. Some loss
before loss of which we fantasize
no possible recovery and draws
us closer, draws us quietly into a
kind of arrest. I've heard *nothing*
described as the absence of degrees
of freedom, the ground state of a
gappd [*sic*] system, by a physicist.
And I wonder if you know what
it means to drive through the desert
not alone, but holding, clutched in
your left hand, loss. Not alone, but
sitting beside something outside of
language, outside of the car, which
nonetheless breathes in and out a
sighing reminder of the temporary.
Wind in the desert leaves its mark
on the pane of your window—dust
makes a layer of summer frost on
which sits the sun and through which
the sun is scattered. O virgin king,
he sighs. He sighs. It's the way the
sun sits in your eyes. She sighs.

Jem

At the top of the mountain was an
ornamental dove, muff-legged and
mute. My eyes have been flooded
with birds from birth, I whispered,
and the sound of ground teeth—my
sister's. Then I knelt and the dove
knelt beside me, opening its mouth
to ask politely my name and kindly
if I would share its own name; silly,
to have forgotten its own name and,
for a moment, its manners and good
breeding. Six hundred blinks from
sundown and without itself, parted
even from the memory of its origin,
lighting itself on fear and forgotten
by its fancier. Bull-eyed derailment,
white as infancy with clipped wings,
tail feathers singed by shale dust,
convulsing from silence. Deafened
birds sing abnormal songs. So they
say. And I'm reminded that I don't
belong here or that I am part ghost-
whisper in the pipes, part belonging.
That I was in this prematurely air-
conditioned super market.

Westmoreland

There is a house in New Orleans
untouched and overlooking bone
in the waters of Pontchartrain and
hedera in the humidity climbing a
poplar whose branches were low
and strong enough to hold the full
weight of three boyhoods in a line
of men. Land in which lay twelve
gauge shells buried next to arrow
heads made of black glass, a spool
of catgut, heels, and the last notes
of a lost trap lord. Where the girl
children born of the house were
each named for a flower and each
born to a season and each beneath
the tree by the same midwife from
the field. Rotting in a knothole are
Mills & Boon yellowbacks hidden
under mildewed roughage and the
afterbirth. Days here go on tedious
and thrown up in light tired for a
long time now like a watch for the
birds which come to live and feed
on the excess, jerking as if broken
from the architecture. The eldest
of these birds, having just escaped
a chicken hawk, bleeding from her
belly, preens her feathers and faces
north for flight.

NORTHERN

♀

You miss your mother. You are always missing your mother. And the people here, they don't understand. You are your mother's child. God made her and she made you and why can't they understand? The people here, they cross the street when they see you, they don't bother to say good morning, they don't bother to reply to your letters, your questions, your texts, your emails. The people here, they are looking through you, practicing for that moment when together they can celebrate your ghost, call you down from heaven, up from hell, tell you they loved you all along. But you're still alive when you learn the name they have for your multiplied nothingness. They whisper and you wonder what delusion it was to have expected even to breathe here. They whisper and you wonder what freedom means. They whisper and you realize this is all there ever was, a screen of faces here and gone from a world lashed to your back. You miss your mother. You are always missing your mother. And the people here, they don't understand that this is all you have, all that survives the fugitive's flight north.

Mikhtam

Set to variations on a normative heartbeat

More and more I turn inward to this sound a steady
rattle and breath parting my bones to build a castle
fortified against what's coming. What walks across
my land is mine to dismiss because there are things
I am afraid

To lose. Things that I know can't be lost in what
opens the luminescent dust of stars through the dark
windows of a place where it's warm. In the vestibule
is briefness and intention. Signature of heat her small
majesty

Holding in her right hand a plush charm, a fetish
against the fugitive light of long expired nebulae. She
reaches backward impossibly and remembers me
where I stand eyes fixed on motion in the glass as
wind slips

in beneath the door with the scent of autumn. She points
and smiles. She offers her plush. She offers that nothing
can harm her.

(Selah)

Lotoux

for Easlin

We have all night said Ankoù,
the heels of his boots like black
bones against the cobblestones,
laughing as we passed at his like
ness in old marble, in one hand
holding roses as light narrowed
and the discussion turned to the
tender tortures of Odilon who,
before the surrealists, saw what
tender palace was Caliban. He
said then that walking through
Rennes was unlike walking on
the oldest parts of Africa, which
had no history, only its weight,
and lay like a dog asleep on the
side of the road. We stopped to
light his cigarette. *Dénicotinisé.*
What's the point I wanted to ask,
but thought not to. We're each
of us running from something
for something we can't none of
us outrun. Nantes is a long way
away and it's been a long time
since I've fallen asleep on your
shoulder thinking of the gambler
our grandmother drank through
and the dead how they dream
dream more vividly of us than
we do of die and gambling men.

Eleanor

in memory of Eleanor Colarusso

New year's day air in the home
is thick with stale piss and bingo
for the old ladies and the one I miss
slouched in her seat not asleep
but bent with regard for a century
lifts her head looking up to get
her bearings clutches a pink plush
to her chest and forgets softness
into an empty stomach rounding
vacancy on the greens of her eyes
after the seasons they disarrange
like rosary beads her prayers each
counted if unnumbered as hours
carry dust   sleep threatens
and nothing bothers her to pause
not the sons not their wives not
her son's one son they never stay
long enough to see her through
one or two moments resting her eyes.
How the present is a fog and what
she remembers a score in years
old the bar that Buddy built
in the basement of the house
in Middle Village the avenue her
girlfriends tenderly stroking each
other's forearms the preserves fresh
produce bagels bread cold cuts
the people she loved. New year's
day and she rests her eyes again

slouches into softness again / hello
sweetheart she says like it was
yesterday like forty winks behind.

Bower

Bharmed and shamed by shiny things
this bounty is a Blood bolony / I think
negus looks like a young king
like Tupac in the mouth and skin
with brude studs in both ears
bubic zirconia how negus wears
the other side of proper / I think
it matters less / we both know / when
he whispers / the train rocking
back and forth brossing the river
between here and home / overdressed
for the warmth of winter / something
about the art of running away / rests
his five-point brown against my sleeve
/ whispers about making this warmth
bolder / ice bold / then pulls back.

Sauvage

for Claire

Quick as red is your concession
to an itch sitting like A.I.
between my mother's fingers
to learn this unrelenting mercy
twisted until lockt in places plaited
3× over a common thread count
diamond cut from the strong hold
of a durational animal bleeding
from the nails / how does it feel
getting in your hair the smell
      rehearsed in oil
lamps through nights lighting
windows across a sleepscape
multitudes wide and more deep
breathing heavy down your neck
heavier than last you remember
when last you sat inside
the star you once wished on
to see what you could see / later
much later kneeling to kiss it.

Cindy

The taste of your breath is
a conversation collapsed into having
no hands half acid half alkali
and realizing the word for anything
might be and this especially
absurd. You're just playing
in the origin of weather's
half live half held gestures
common if uncommitted
and rolling into this film
on fantasy which begat me
a stock without foot on the floor
of a feast in my honor the music
lost when the people had gone
and the hall a wreck and just
us left like a stiff wind makes a softer
nothing a fire makes clean
the myth of you spitting seeds.

Minerva

To expect   / worse   / ask
your glimpse of God still learning
the color of Mars to be kind
of a tone other than dictated
by note is not a lost cause / really /
glacial is how we used to describe
the pace a body needs to make
clarion every labored odor
stressed from pores and pores
in the bark of a memory of a mark
on the small of someone's back /
though a fool or a faith healer
waiting with ears pricked for the sound
of a new world born between breaths
this might make you / crack open
like an éclair tongued for its cream.

Rasheed

in memory of Rasheed Thurmond

I did in the desert I ate death been dying
ever since straining for the taste of a need
to know something about the nervous life
of my left arm dumb sensitive and how
much is the 40 oz for a man who knew
no fear a man on in years who walked out
the desert more than alive once more
than they say ecstatic crown in the county
cocked to the side and smiling these are
the seraphim these are the holy of Kings.

Taylor

You look unhappy she said extended
a feverish hand trying not to constrain
two palaces impressed by the human
timbre of the mark I sat on her face
book swimming chills up and down
a need in me to thrash holy_my tongue
in jars and jars of the same hive's honey
(sweet ((rawr)) honey) getting tired
and self-conscious finally overcome
when someone pulls me off the bees
dims the screen sings undershepherd
all slick then foamy and exclaiming
there's a picture of you somewhere
posing in a Power Rangers costume
and can I see   which color is you

    baby I promise- -I promise you
have nothing I want.

Alborada

If by then the sun
has risen on us still sleep
your skin a coolness
                              asked
to stay the night-sputter
of your shoulder tucked
beneath the lie of my chin
crossing the dark stutter
of your dreams your palms
having found their way in
to the nerve-sweat of my own
& mercy for the mutter-
psalm you seem to chuff
folded between my arms
(holding so you sleep enough
& I sleep eventually) after
you've pressed the song-weight
of your name into the spoon
of my chest where what stirs
is water want for knowledge
of the sea that separates me
from the world you turn
& say in your mother tongue
good morning.

Blerim

I'm learning to eat for days ahead
to rock myself humming to sleep
to tend exhaustions I haven't bathed
in in weeks with gum in good-bye weather
as the train over the bridge rocks me closer
chewing a city given in good-bye light
its shape I carry tuning for one channel
peopled quiet not to fail the memory
of Mommy rocking me to sleep forget
not to insist I learned so young to hear
everything she showed me dreaming
the sky how soon I knew this flying
as my inner ear.

Call me kin to the lone heads
nodding lions sleep on lines
rocking underground over
world all hours passages
back back home going home
back home home / come home
like that / back / back home /
come home / come back home

Notes

"Aleta"   When asked for a definition of "nothing" (by Neil Degrasse Tyson), Eva Silverstein, professor of physics at Stanford University, replied: ". . . the absence of degrees of freedom . . . The ground state of a gapped quantum system."

"Jem"   "I was in this prematurely air-conditioned super market" is from a lyric by Lucinda Childs featured in *Einstein on the Beach*.

"Westmoreland"   "There is a house in New Orleans" is from the song "House of the Rising Sun."

Acknowledgments

"Monkey Study with Fur" owes a debt of gratitude to Patricio Ferrari for providing facsimiles of Fernando Pessoa's English language poetry.

"Blerim" was published in *Obsidian: Literature & Arts in the African Diaspora* 43, no. 1 (Spring 2017).

Andrew E. Colarusso is the author of *The Sovereign* (Dalkey Archive Press, 2017). He was editor in chief of *The Broome Street Review* from 2009 to 2017.